The White House

Julie Murray

abdopublishing.com

Published by Abdo Kids, a division of ABDO, PO Box 398166, Minneapolis, Minnesota 55439.
Copyright © 2017 by Abdo Consulting Group, Inc. International copyrights reserved in all countries.
No part of this book may be reproduced in any form without written permission from the publisher.

Printed in the United States of America, North Mankato, Minnesota.

102016

012017

THIS BOOK CONTAINS
RECYCLED MATERIALS

Photo Credits: Alamy, iStock, John F. Kennedy Library, Library of Congress, The White House, Shutterstock,
©Ryan Somma p.13 / CC-BY-2.0, ©Ritu Manoj Jethani p.23 / Shutterstock.com

Production Contributors: Teddy Borth, Jennie Forsberg, Grace Hansen

Design Contributors: Christina Doffing, Candice Keimig, Dorothy Toth

Publisher's Cataloging in Publication Data

Names: Murray, Julie, author.

Title: The White House / by Julie Murray.

Description: Minneapolis, Minnesota : Abdo Kids, 2017 | Series: US landmarks |
    Includes bibliographical references and index.

Identifiers: LCCN 2016944076 | ISBN 9781680809169 (lib. bdg.) |
    ISBN 9781680796261 (ebook) | ISBN 9781680796933 (Read-to-me ebook)

Subjects: LCSH: White House (Washington, D.C.)--Juvenile literature. |
    Washington (D.C.)--Buildings, structures, etc.--Juvenile literature.

Classification: DDC 975.3--dc23

LC record available at http://lccn.loc.gov/2016944076

Table of Contents

It is in Washington **D.C.**

It is more than 200 years old.

It is white. It is big!

It has 132 rooms.

13

The president works in the Oval Office.

You can take a **tour** of the White House.

It is an important

US **Landmark**.

Have you seen the

White House?

More Rooms in the White House

Blue Room

Red Room

Green Room

Yellow Room

Glossary

D.C.
short for District of Columbia.

landmark
a preserved place that has cultural importance and status.

tour
a short trip through or around a place in order to view it.

Index

abdokids.com

Use this code to log on to abdokids.com and access crafts, games, videos, and more!

Abdo Kids Code:
UTK9169